LISTEN
TO SUCCEED

LESLIE B. SHORE

*How to identify and overcome
barriers to effective listening*

© 2012 Leslie B. Shore

Copyright © 2012 by Leslie B. Shore
Printed in U.S.
Library of Congress Cataloging-in-Publication Date

Editor: Evelyn B. Shore
Illustrator: Paula Leckey

ISBN-13 978 1475282269
ISBN-10 1475282265

Content Information Note

Names of persons appearing in this book in boxed items as authors of case studies are fictitious.

ACKNOWLEDGEMENTS

MY SINCERE GRATITUDE to Evelyn B. Shore, editor extraordinaire, for her patience and wisdom and to Michelle Silverman who has been an integral part of this fifteen-year listening journey.

My appreciation to Professor Carole Gesme who believed my work in listening had a readership far beyond the university walls. My thanks also to secondary school instructor Sara Foose Parrott, PhD, who saw within me the teacher I would become.

Many thanks to my readers, Fred Bartling, PhD; Lynn Riskedal, PhD; Anne Peak, JD; Craig Shore; John Rozman; Katherine Waymire; Holli Rietmulder; John Capecci, PhD; as well as Maurice Shore; Ron Berg; and Mark Morton for their essential feedback.

I also honor here my grandmother Sadie Greenberg Bennett, whose legacy of listening is the basis of this work, and my father, David N. Shore, who lived listening as a way of being.

TABLE OF CONTENTS

INTRODUCTION

MY WORK ON LISTENING BEGAN when I reflected on why my grandmother was so successful at building relationships with her family, her friends, and people she met. Why did people change their demeanor in a positive way when they spoke with her? Why did her fellow residents always flock to her apartment to talk? Why did her granddaughter (me) look forward to Saturday afternoons together? Why? Because my grandmother had mastered the art and skill of listening effectively. Everyone was special to her, so she listened with total concentration and sincerity and remembered what everyone had to say. People loved her because, by listening to them day in and day out, without reservation, she showed them how much she cared and valued them. When I looked at successful people in all areas of my life, I began to see the same skill.

How do longtime CEOs stay at the top? How do athletes and coaches enjoy such long careers? How do actors and directors continue to make a multitude of successful films? How do inventors continually come up with new products? How do long-married couples stay married? What do parents do to bring up well-adjusted children? What keeps salespeople at the top of their game? The skill of listening effectively! Though all of these groups of people have different talents and skills, they all have one skill in common, the ability to listen effectively.

These effective listeners understand that listening does *not* mean just waiting for our turn to respond. They understand that listening effectively is the key to increased knowledge, emotional intelligence, business success, career mobility, and productive and growing relationships. As effective listeners they have learned to put aside their egos and attend to the person they are listening to.

This book will show how we too can build on the listener we already are and become a highly-skilled and more effective one. When we've completed *Listen to Succeed* and seen the results of its companion, the *Listening Effectiveness Profile*, we'll then know, with little doubt, where we stand as a listener now and how we can move to where we want to be.

> *Courage is what it takes to stand up and speak;*
> *courage is also what it takes to sit down and listen.*
> —Winston Churchill

CHAPTER ONE

THE IMPORTANCE OF LISTENING

"I only wish I could find an institute that teaches people how to listen. Business people need to listen at least as much as they need to talk. Too many people fail to realize that real communication goes in both directions."

— Lee Iacocca

IMAGINE A WORLD where every world leader, parent, teacher, manager, and friend has become an effective listener. What would a world populated with truly effective listeners be like? How would it be different? In this kind of world, conversations would not lead to arguments; discussions would not escalate into altercations; and everyone would thoroughly listen to what a speaker had to say in order to understand what was said the *first* time it was spoken.

What Is "Listening"?

Many people believe that hearing and listening are the same, but they are not. Hearing is merely the physical reception of sound. Listening is the attachment of meaning to sound through knowledge and experience.

Hearing is passive and automatic. Unless our hearing is impeded for some reason (hearing impairment, protective devices or ear plugs, background noise or distractions), we hear sounds whether we're trying to receive them or not. *Listening, on the other hand, is active and intentional.* It involves three functions: hearing, processing the message, and reacting to it either through words or body postures.

Listening does not occur automatically. It's the result of a conscious choice we make, just as we can make a conscious decision *not* to listen.

We often spend only enough time and energy to hear without taking the time to listen. Whether in our personal or professional life, we now do more multitasking, experience more technology interruptions, and fall victim to far more stress caused by a jam-packed schedule than ever before. But understanding the difference between hearing and listening is an important prerequisite for listening effectively, and listening effectively is the key to success in all areas of life.

Why Is Listening So Important?

Though the answer to this question may seem obvious, it really isn't. Ready answers might be…

"So I can do the job right."

"So I can learn from the person talking."

"So I can see what is bothering my teenager."

"So I can be on top of my game at work."

Although these answers are right, they only scratch the surface. We are working and living today in a "knowledge economy." Personal and professional success leans heavily on how much we can learn about our friends and family, our jobs, the organizations where we work, and ourselves. Applying that knowledge to new situations through our *effective* listening skills helps us not only to increase our own knowledge but to handle ourselves in the world around us as well.

Learning to listen effectively calls for developing a certain set of skills; and it's important to acknowledge to ourselves that, even though our skills may be well developed, they can weaken without practice. Regardless of current capabilities, all listeners can continue to improve through practice, practice, practice.

Listening and Self-Esteem

Before we consider the multitude of benefits we get from listening effectively, a good place for us to start our journey is by looking at ourselves and the kind of listeners we are *now*. The reality is that the reasons for becoming a more effective listener reach deep down into our own self-esteem needs and those of the people we're listening to.

Take a look at the two questions asked of hundreds of participants in my Listening Effectiveness Seminar and the responses they described.

1. **How do you feel when you know you are *not* being listened to?**

Ignored	Disrespected
Frustrated	Unimportant
Not valued	Irritated
Angry	Disconnected
Alone	Insecure
Invisible	Disappointed

We can see that many of the sentiments expressed above relate directly to a speaker's emotional well-being. Not being listened to creates significant negative emotions in us, often leaving us feeling unwelcome, unsafe, unappreciated, and devalued, all of which strike at the core of one's self-esteem. We may have experienced these negative feelings ourselves when we were talking to someone who was not listening, and the feeling of not really having been heard could easily have returned us to our most insecure places.

As listeners, therefore, we hold a tremendous amount of power in deciding how a conversation will proceed. Only through thoughtfully paying attention to the speaker can creative, forward-thinking responses and lively conversation take place. If we're not attentive, not only does the speaker feel devalued, but we put significant limits on our own capacity to learn and grow.

We give speakers a number of visual clues that let them know we're not really listening, including:
- Failing to make eye contact.
- Using closed or defensive body postures.

- Engaging in other activities that take concentration, like reading or texting on a smartphone.
- Not nodding as a silent response saying "I see" or "Ah-ha."

Now let's look at listening from a different perspective. Note the responses to the other question from my Listening Effectiveness Seminar.

....

2. How do you feel when you know you are being listened to?

Valued	Appreciated
Loved	Content
Involved	Intelligent
Welcome	Rescued
Relaxed	Secure

....

These were the words the participants used, but what others could we add? Just imagine how instrumental we might be as listeners if we could change the visual and other cues we give to speakers and create an engaging environment for the speaker, one that makes the most out of the exchange we are involved in.

If the feelings above are how positive we feel when we're being listened to, think about the positive role we could play if we let speakers know we are listening to them.

What Is "Effective Listening"?

When we listen *effectively*, we are activating a skill. We understand the content and meaning of what the speaker is saying and are able to put what was said into our own words. We can then show the speaker, through our responses, that we've understood the intent and the content of the message from the speaker's perspective.

When we listen effectively:

- Cooperation is increased because speakers can see that their input is valued.

- Better decisions are made because information is accumulated from multiple sources.
- Conflict is lessened because misunderstandings and misconceptions are avoided or caught more quickly.
- Costly errors are prevented because we've heard and processed information and had feedback from all stakeholders.
- The speaker's level of openness increases, allowing for deeper conversations and connection.

There are four major components to effective listening:

- Being present.
- Taking in information from others while being nonjudgmental.
- Acknowledging the speaker in a way that invites communication to continue.
- Waiting for the period at the end of the speaker's sentence before formulating a reply.

If we use all four components simultaneously, we're listening effectively! Here's a quick look at each component:

Being Present

Being "present" is a simple concept, but a difficult one to achieve. Being present is the act of being in the present moment in our mind and body, not thinking about the past or the future, but *being in the moment* with the person we are listening to. Being present means we're not comparing the speaker or the message with anything or anyone else, and we're not wishing we could be somewhere else. Being present means practicing self-control, suppressing the urge to convey our own thoughts. Being present means not focusing on ourselves but concentrating on understanding what the speaker has to say instead. Effective listeners, those who are in the moment and focused on the speaker, receive, welcome, and remain free to accept the communication as it's offered.

> *"As a manager, I am required to constantly interact with others every day. When I come home at the end of the day, I want nothing more than to read my e-mails and browse the web for the latest news. I want nothing more than to sit in silence without the requirement to listen.*
> *My wife, however, wants nothing more than to tell me about her day, and so the listening challenge begins. Yes, being an effective listener does require sacrifice.*
> *While I have previously heard her talk, I realize now that I have not really listened. I have allowed the preoccupation with my daily routine to get in the way of my ability to be present to what my wife's thoughts and emotions are.*
> *Unfortunately, this selfishness is not confined to my personal life. I can also be preoccupied at work with finalizing a proposal, sending an e-mail, or any of the other myriad tasks I must accomplish within a day.*

*My commitment to release myself from such
preoccupations is an absolute requirement if I am to
become an effective listener."*

— Robert

Taking in Information from Others While Being Nonjudgmental

Listening to what others have to say can be a difficult task. As we will find out, being judgmental is one of the major barriers standing in the way of effective listening. If we are to receive a speaker's intended message in unadulterated form, it is essential that we remove judgment from our listening process while the speaker is speaking. On-the-spot judgments about what we're hearing doesn't benefit us or the speaker. When we're reactive or defensive, we cannot listen. We need to set aside our egos, our biases, and our inner thoughts so that we don't filter the speaker's message until we've had time to consider it. This type of listening is highly reflective; it allows us to process the speaker's communication first before we use our own experience and knowledge to create a reply.

*"I consider my coworker to have a higher socio-
economic status than I have in terms of income,
education, and occupation. Because of this, I simply*

cannot listen to what she says without bias. When she talks about having to "budget" since enrolling her infant in a nursery school, I immediately assume that she has no idea of what it is really like to have to live on a budget. Don't get me wrong. I know that she has worked hard to get where she is today, but I always dismiss what she talks about based on my preconceived opinion of her socio-economic status."

— Jessi

Acknowledging the Speaker in a Way That Invites Communication to Continue

When we show no visible reaction to what we're hearing, it can be easy for the speaker to assume that we're either not listening, not understanding what we're hearing, or not comfortable with the message we're getting. This kind of misunderstanding stops the free flow of information. No matter what reasons we may have for not reacting, we are responsible for our listening. We need to acknowledge the speaker in a way that tells the speaker we *are* listening.

Speakers can interpret facial expressions in any number of ways (interested, quizzical, earnest, bored). They can also read our body language in the form of posture, gestures, and head movements. Simply making comments along the lines of "wow," "ah-ha," "hmm," or "I see" acknowledges the speaker and lets him or her know that we're listening. Without acknowledgment, speakers can feel invisible and not listened to; but with appropriate acknowledgment, they can tell that their message is coming across and how we're receiving it.

> *"As a marriage counselor, I hear the same stories over and over again and find it difficult to stay engaged. My normal form of acknowledgment is a raised eyebrow, a nod, or a simple, "I understand." But I find that when I don't actively acknowledge my clients as they are speaking, they shut down quickly. They assume correctly that I am not listening to them carefully. I've recently realized I can do more to remodel my listening behavior in a way my clients could use in their relationships."*
>
> — Diane

Waiting for the Period at the End of the Speaker's Sentence before Formulating a Reply

The most difficult component of listening effectively seems to be *waiting for the period at the end of the sentence before formulating a reply*. Kenneth Wells, the former CEO of General Motors writes, "A good listener tries to understand what the other person is saying. In the end he may disagree sharply; but because he disagrees, he wants to know exactly what it is he is disagreeing with."[1]

---

1   Kenneth Wells, Guide to Good Leadership (Chicago: Science Research Associates, 1956).

The only way we can know what we are disagreeing *with* is to listen all the way through to the end of the sentence or the thought that has been expressed. When we begin working on a reply before the speaker is finished, we lose both the complete information being offered and an understanding of the kind of emotion present in the speaker's delivery. We unilaterally decide that what we're thinking about as a reply is more important than what the listener has been saying. We are fully engaged in the process of putting our own thoughts and ourselves first without giving the speaker a complete hearing. Many misunderstandings and communication conflicts can arise when the listener is too involved in preparing a response to really listen to what's been said.

> *"When we deliberate as a group, I think I may not be completely invested in listening to people as they are speaking to me. Meaning, I am often thinking about my response to what is being said, not listening intently to what is being presented. Holding my responses and suspending*

*my own thoughts until the end of the presented
information is challenging. I occasionally catch
myself creating responses before the speaker is
completely finished."*

—Josh

Keys to Effective Listening

The key to becoming an effective listener lies in recognizing that there are barriers standing in the way of our ability to listen fully. Using our knowledge of how to deal with these barriers can become an important pathway to our personal and professional success. We need only to look at technology and our own sensory skills of seeing and hearing to recognize some of these barriers to listening effectively. Information overload like telephones ringing, e-mails popping up on the monitor, and text message alerts beeping, creates a formidable barrier to our effective listening. It can border on impossible to focus entirely on what's being said to us when there's so much noise around. But there are many other kinds of barrier too, all of them fighting for our attention and concentration and challenging our ability to listen effectively.

Because listening is a single-minded, reasoning task, multi-tasking and listening effectively at the same time are mutually exclusive. From Eyal Ophir, a researcher at Stanford University's Communication Between Humans and Interactive Media Lab, we have learned that "The human mind is not really built for processing multiple streams of information. The ability to process a second stream of information is really limited."[2]

In order to develop mastery over barriers like information overload and to acknowledge our inability to process multiple streams of information, we must first understand that we are continually being challenged by two kinds of listening barriers: *external* and *internal*. Each type of barrier can prevent us from listening effectively; but once we recognize each, we can use our awareness to develop an improvement plan that will benefit both our personal and our occupational goals.

As we move forward, we will never see terms like "good," "bad," "better," or "worse" to describe the level of the listening skills we have now. The listeners we are now are the result of who our models have been in the past. We didn't choose our parents, the

2   Eyal Ophir, Proceedings of the National Academy of Sciences (Psychology Press, 1999).

extended family we were born into, or the culture we came from. Our listening skills have been largely determined by what we have learned so far from those skills modeled by family, friends, teachers, bosses, and other people who have influenced our life. But with this book, we have an opportunity to examine not only how we're listening today but how we can create a new listening model for the future.

Putting Effective Listening into Action

Now that we know *why* we need to listen effectively, we need to discover *what* can get in the way. Current culture seems to contribute to our being passive listeners rather than active ones. We've been conditioned to rely on the speaker of the message to motivate us to listen; we've put the burden on the speaker instead of taking responsibility ourselves. Yet it's up to us as the listeners, rather than the speaker, *to work with each spoken message we receive as we are receiving it* in order to benefit from it. To do that, we need to understand the nature of the barriers that might be getting in our way.

Even though we want to listen effectively, barriers tend to stop us from being the best listeners we can be. They may stem directly from how we were listened to by parents and teachers while we were growing up, or they may come from experiences we have had as adults in the working world. Our barriers to listening effectively normally go undetected; but once we're aware of them, we can choose to temporarily deactivate them.

In the next two chapters, we will familiarize ourselves with the kinds of external and internal barriers that impede effective listening, and we'll also look at steps we can take to overcome them.

CHAPTER TWO

EXTERNAL LISTENING BARRIERS

EXTERNAL LISTENING BARRIERS cover a wide range of issues and situations. They involve our senses of hearing, seeing, and smelling, as well as issues of comfort. Within each larger barrier are a number of smaller identifiable obstacles that we may or may not be able to specifically relate to.

External barriers consist of *outside actions* that affect us and draw our attention away from the speaker in a listening situation. Because these barriers may have been in place for years, it is rare for us to be able to completely eradicate them. However, we can certainly use our new awareness of their existence in order to be a consistently effective listener. Just as we are able to do with any other skill-based activity, we can become acutely aware of what our own external listening barriers are and how we can overcome them. We will discover the many ways in which each barrier can negatively affect our listening, how we can tell which barrier is affecting us, and which strategy we can use to alleviate it and listen effectively. The three listening obstructions we will examine here are: *hearing barriers, visual barriers,* and *physically affective barriers.*

Hearing Barriers

How well can we *hear* a speaker in any situation? Are there distractions coming from the physical environment that keep us from listening effectively?

Hearing barriers include noise, poor acoustics, and aspects of a speaker's delivery that don't involve the actual words spoken but the method of emphasis and shades of meaning given to what is being said.

Noise

Noise is a distraction with a wide range. It can be as soft as a tapping pencil, as loud as an air conditioner, or as intrusive as construction taking place outside a restaurant where we're dining with friends. It also becomes more difficult to listen effectively the closer we are to the source of the noise.

Noise can be intermittent or constant. Intermittent noise includes clocks ticking, jackhammering, constant coughing, and loud telephone conversations. These sounds are difficult to ignore. They disrupt our ability to listen because they're non-rhythmic, break our concentration, and make it difficult to effectively listen.

On the other hand, constant noise, like air conditioning or the continuous babble in an office environment, forces us to spend considerable energy trying to tune out the sound or push it into the background.

No matter what the nature of the noise is, the moment we focus on it, we've stopped listening. Thoughts like, "I wish she wouldn't crack her knuckles" or "It's noisy in here" are telling us the noise barrier has the upper hand over our listening. To counteract noise distractions like these, we need to increase our levels of concentration and energy.

NOISE: POSSIBLE SOLUTIONS
If noise is one of my listening barriers, I could:
- Acknowledge how distracting the noise is to me.
- Ask the speaker for a change of place if the situation allows it.
- Arrange for meetings to be in locations I know to be quiet.
- Postpone the conversation if the noise is too distracting.
- Try deep breathing and refocusing.

Acoustics

Acoustics has to do with the sound quality of a room, with how effectively a space can reflect sound waves that produce clear hearing. There are times when a room's sound delivery system or physical construction, such as poor speaker placement, can prevent listeners from being able to hear well. Speech may be muffled or garbled; the microphone may give feedback or fail to project sufficiently; or the normal range of speech may not come through sharply enough because of a poor sound system.

When we're spending most of our energy and concentration just trying to hear in a poor acoustic situation, there's not much energy left to listen. We can't hear well enough to process the verbal part of the message, and it leads to misunderstandings.

We know we've hit an acoustic listening barrier when we're straining to hear clearly even though other types of noise barriers already mentioned are absent. We're thinking, "I can't make out what the speaker is saying" or "I wish I knew how to read lips."

ACOUSTICS: POSSIBLE SOLUTIONS

If acoustics is one of my listening barriers, I could:

- Move my location so I can see the speaker's lips move as an aid to my listening.
- Move to be closer to the speaker, away from the amplifier, or out of range of the noise in some other way.

Speaker Delivery

Many times, it's the speaker's way of speaking that creates a barrier for us. The speaker's voice is:

- Too loud or soft, causing us to either back away or strain forward to catch the message.

- Too rapid or slow, causing us stress or boredom.
- Without inflection, being neither raised nor lowered so as to indicate what the speaker feels is important.

When we struggle with the speaker's delivery, our concentration is divided. No matter how valuable the message is, the manner and method of its delivery can prevent us from listening effectively to the content. We know we've hit the speaker delivery barrier when we're thinking "I wish they would speak up" or "Could they pick up the speed?" or "I can't figure out what's important."

> **SPEAKER DELIVERY: POSSIBLE SOLUTIONS**
> If speaker delivery is one of my listening barriers, I could:
> - Ask the speaker to speak up or slow down.
> - Stay engaged by taking notes using the speaker's keywords in preparation for asking questions.

Nonverbal Language

Nonverbal language refers to the sound patterns speakers use to deliver a message. We are often able to sense a speaker's attitude from the way he or she uses voice to add emphasis or shades of meaning to the message.

Nonverbal language consists of four components:

1. *Voice quality*—Pitch (moving from higher to lower octaves), clear or mumbling transitions between words, sharp or relaxed pronunciation, even or uneven emphasis on words, and richness or thinness of the voice.
2. *Vocal characterization*—Sounds, other than words, used to create meaning, such as heavy sighs, clearing of the throat, yawning, laughing, or audibly inhaling and exhaling.
3. *Fillers*—Nonwords such as "um," "uh," or "uh-huh."
4. *Timing*—The pace of speech delivery and duration of silences and pauses.

Although these vocal cues give us a great deal of information about what the speaker is truly conveying, we may not be bothering to listen to and interpret them. For example, when the speaker uses the vocal filler "um" an inordinate number of times and we become distracted by it, we might miss the fact that the speaker is either nervous or not comfortable with what he or she is saying. When we do not listen to and understand the timing, silence, or pauses the speaker is using to emphasize a point, we can miss the full meaning of the message. In cases like this, an understanding of nonverbal language can give us more insight into the speaker and the speaker's message.

Whenever we feel that there's more to the message than the speaker's words or body language suggest, we may ask ourselves questions like, "Why are they slowing down?" or "What are they trying to say by raising their voice an octave?" We feel the message is somehow being manipulated on a subconscious level, but we're not sure what the reason is.

> ### NONVERBAL LANGUAGE: POSSIBLE SOLUTIONS
> If nonverbal language is one of my listening barriers, I could:
> - Spend some time watching speeches on the Internet to see how nonverbal language adds to, detracts from, or changes the meaning of speech.
> - Notice when the speaker is using certain forms of nonverbal language: tone, sound of voice, nonverbal sounds, or delivery speed.

Ways to Alleviate Hearing Barriers

Move

If there's nothing we can do about the poor acoustics or other hearing barriers, there are still steps we can take to ensure the best listening possible. We can move to a place where we can see the speaker's lips. We may be able to fill in what we can't hear with what we can see on the speaker's lips.

Ask

As nicely as possible, ask the speaker to slow down or speak up. Our request shows the speaker respect by making it clear we want to hear what's being said; and if the speaker obliges, we get the intended message because our mind is not wandering.

Observe

If we're feeling confused because the speaker's words do not match the delivery, we need to look for paralinguistic cues. For example, if the subject matter is exciting and the speaker's voice is a monotone, we gain insight into the speaker's underlying attitude or state (tired, nervous, distracted).

Visual Barriers

Visual barriers consist of distractions not just right next to us but anywhere in our line of sight. We can be distracted from listening effectively by simply catching sight of something interesting or by a speaker's body language and the assumptions we might be making about it.

Although our intent is to listen effectively, our eyes are always taking in visual information at the same time we're listening. Because visual distractions can impede our ability to listen, we need to be aware of the types of visual barriers there are so we can overcome them. We can look at visual barriers from two different points of view, first from a *general* point of view and secondly from a *focused* point of view

Visual Barriers: The General View

General viewing comprises sights that are in front of us, either *inactive objects* like a bookcase or a statue or *active figures* like a flying bird or a latecomer entering a meeting. In both of these situations, we are free to pay attention to these sights at random, allowing them to become barriers to receiving the message the speaker is delivering. The extent to which *general views* are distracting is always contingent on the amount of attention we decide to pay to them. Here are a few examples:

Inactive Visual Distractions	*Active Visual Distractions*
Bulletin board with notices on it	Passersby on a busy street
Wall mural	Moving vehicles
Street signs	Lightning

In actual cases like the ones above, our listening-viewing brains are required to attend to the words we're hearing while processing the distracting visual information we're receiving at the same time. What we're seeing competes with what we're trying to listen to, and we end up unable to fully receive the speaker's message.

Inactive visual barrier   *Active visual barriers*

*"I have always had issues with active visual
distractions, like people walking by my classroom,
sitting in a restaurant facing into the restaurant, or
even talking at a party where I could see everything
that was happening. It was severely affecting my
ability to listen. My brain was being split in two,
trying to multitask all I was seeing and hearing. As
a result, I was not listening effectively. I now choose
my seat as quickly as possible to ensure I will listen.
I actually maneuver where I will be facing when in
conversations at social gatherings."*

— Kathryn

Ways to Alleviate General View Barriers

Whether standing or seated, we can always attempt to change
our position. If we're distracted when people walk by during a
meeting, we can always try to change where we sit. If we're at a

restaurant and we're being distracted by the activity of the open room, we need to change position to face away from the activity. When we ask others to accommodate these needs, we need to tell them why. Our speakers will appreciate that we cared enough to want to listen effectively.

> **GENERAL VIEW: POSSIBLE SOLUTIONS**
> If the general view is one of my listening barriers, I could:
> - Arrive early so I have my pick of available seating and choose a seat that allows for the least amount of distraction.
> - Face away from the activity of the party. Let others know I'm moving so I can listen more effectively.

Visual Barriers: The Focused View

Once our visual attention rests on the speaker alone, we are in *focused view,* observing only the nonverbal communication we get from the speaker. *Body language* becomes the primary nonverbal communication we receive through the speaker's facial expressions, eye behavior, gestures, posture, and closeness or distance. Much of body language is involuntary, and, as such, it's very difficult for a speaker to control the movement of every part of the body at the same time.

Body language adds to the meaning of the words being delivered. It conveys messages about the emotional truth of the communication. We make judgments about other people, sometimes subconsciously, aided by our understanding of the body language of the person in question. There are times when we find ourselves liking, disliking, or even mistrusting a speaker, often without knowing why. Therefore, when listening, paying close attention to the body language of the person is a must. A nonverbal message can reinforce or contradict the verbal message we're getting. If we can't recognize the body language for what it is and see a disparity between the verbal and nonverbal messages we're receiving, we're depriving ourselves of a clear picture of what the speaker *really* means.

In this book, the particular body language discussed is rooted in the Western/European tradition. However, it is important for us to remember that there are wide cultural differences as to what body language means. Our world is increasingly diverse, and people of different backgrounds come together to speak and be heard.

What follows are eight basic areas of Western body language we can watch that should aid us in becoming more effective listeners: touch, eye contact, facial expression, head position, gesture, posture, distance, and body motion.

Touch

Touching between the speaker and the listener can occur. Some typical occurrences are professional, such as doctor with patient; social, such as a handshake; and approving, such as a pat on the back. How appropriate is the contact? Do we understand our response to what the speaker is conveying with the contact?

Eye Contact

The eyes can seek information, show interest, dominate others, invite or control interaction, provide feedback, and reveal attitudes. The amount of eye contact and its intensity say a great deal about how we respond to the speaker in the moment. Is the eye contact conveying interest and thoughtfulness? Or is the speaker employing the "thousand-yard stare" with unfocused eyes and energy? Do we understand what the eye contact is saying? Is the eye contact "in sync" with what the speaker is communicating verbally? Or, is eye contact blocked in some way?

We can't have eye contact if we can't see each other's eyes, so sometimes we may need to remove sunglasses, for example, or ask the person we're speaking with to do the same.

What is he really thinking?

Facial Expressions

Facial cues are one of the most important sources of nonverbal communication because our faces can reveal many of our thoughts and emotions. There are certain basic facial expressions that we cannot control no matter how hard we try. They come from a core of emotions - happy, sad, disgusted, angry, afraid, or interested, among others. If we are to listen effectively, we need to interpret instantaneously the speaker's facial expressions. Do we understand these facial expressions, and are they at odds with what the speaker is saying?

> *"An in-law we often visit would smile, give us gifts,*
> *and act like she wanted to be one of our dearest*
> *friends. When I commented on how nicely she*
> *treated us, my husband surprised me by saying,*
> *"Her eyes never smile." The next time we saw her, I*
> *watched her eyes and sure enough: they were cold*
> *and flat. It was very disconcerting. I don't know why*
> *her eyes do that, or what it means, but evidently she*
> *can smile at will."*
>
> — Cheri

Head Positions

There are basic head positions that can tell the listener how the speaker feels about the response a listener is giving. If the speaker's head is straight up and forward, the speaker feels neutral about what is being said. If the head is tilted to one side, the speaker is interested in what is being said; but if the tilt is combined with a defensive pulling back, it may indicate suspicion. Tilting can also indicate curiosity or uncertainty, especially when the head is pushed forward as if the speaker were trying to look at the responder in a different way, hoping to hear something new. The speaker's head facing forward with the chin down but the eyes forward shows disapproval, and a lowered head with eyes lowered is usually a speaker's defensive position, indicating a perceived threat.

Gestures

There are two kinds of gestures to look for when we listen to a speaker, *conscious* and *unconscious*.

Conscious gestures consist of those the speaker intentionally employs to emphasize, motivate, or teach, among other goals. When a person is passionate about a subject, these gestures can nonverbally convey purpose and intent behind words.

- Nods of the head.
- OK hand gesture.
- Military salute.

Unconscious gestures are those we make without thinking, and they can reveal a speaker's true feelings. Below are some common unconscious gestures and their possible meanings:

- Open hands show friendliness.
- Hiding of hands may show guilt.
- Biting fingernails shows nervousness.
- Closed fists show defensiveness or aggression.
- Hand to cheek shows contemplation.
- Ankles crossed may mean withholding of information.
- Drumming the fingers shows nervousness or boredom.
- Leaning forward shows interest.
- Tapping feet shows nervousness or lying.
- Crossed arms show defensiveness and objection to what's being heard.

It's important for us to know that what we recognize as acceptable gestures in the United States are not always understood and correctly interpreted universally. What may be understood or considered appropriate in one culture may be rude or even obscene in another one.

Posture

For an observant listener, how speakers hold their body while sitting and standing is one of the first clues we have to their personality and emotional state. Posture reflects an underlying state of mind. People who are feeling hopeful, assured, or dominant will generally adopt more erect postures while those who are feeling depressed, shy, or submissive tend to assume a collapsed, slouched position.

There are other postures that convey meaning as well:

- Hands on knees shows readiness.
- Hands on hips shows impatience or anger.
- Hands behind the back shows self-control.
- Hands behind the head shows confidence.
- Sitting with a leg over the arm of the chair suggests indifference.
- Legs or feet pointed in a particular direction suggest where the greater interest is felt.

Distance

The use of space and distance has the ability to convey power, control, interest, and sincerity for both speaker and listener. Therefore, the physical space between listener and speaker has the capacity to change the dynamics of how we listen. Where we sit and where we stand in relation to one another is no small matter.

Distance While Seated

"Where do you want to sit?" is a loaded question. It's surprising how where we sit actually sends an important message. When we go to sit at a table, our choice can change both the dynamic of the conversation and our ability to listen. Take into consideration the seating diagrams that follow. We can sometimes choose our own seating, and we can do it with full knowledge of its effect on our listening.

Competitive seating

Seats are arranged so participants sit directly across from each other. Here, a desk or table between opposing parties can deliberately create safe space and possibly assist both sides. On the other hand, the distance between the participants may prove to be too hard to  overcome, or undesirable in some other way, and lead to less than optimal listening. Examples where this type of proximity can matter are interviews, negative performance reviews, and deliberations with opposing parties.

Cooperative seating

Seats are arranged so participants sit with just a corner of the desk or table between them. The participants feel safe with each other. The interpersonal space is closer, making it easier to listen to each other, to have eye contact, and to watch body language. There is less chance for miscommunication.

Modified cooperative seating

Seats are arranged so participants sit side by side, allowing for sharing needed resources and permitting almost effortless communication to complete a task.

Co-active seating

Seats are arranged to achieve a distance between the participants in which little communication is desired. It allows for eye contact when needed and permits effective listening to take place as well.

Seating in the Round

Seats are arranged based on a circular placement of chairs. With an in-the-round arrangement, participants have maximum eye contact.

> *"The significance of the Round Table was that no one person, not even King Arthur, would be able to sit at the head of such a table. A round table enforced the concept of equality amongst the Knights of the Round Table. The legend states that King Arthur ordered the Round Table to be built in order to resolve a conflict among his knights concerning who should have precedence. The Round Table was therefore built to ensure that all the Knights of the Round Table were deemed equal and every one of the seats at the Round Table were all seen as highly favored places."*
>
> — Medieval Life and Times

Each one of these seating arrangements changes the proximity of one person to another and changes the listening dynamic at the same time. The ease of making eye contact and observing body language, and the sense of power participants can feel over each other, all influence how effectively listeners and speakers can interact.

Distance While Seated or Standing

We all have "bubbles" around us that we consider to be our intimate, personal, social, and public space. When someone encroaches on our intimate or personal domain or space, our ability and desire to communicate and listen changes.

The amount of space between speaker and listener can make conversation either comfortable or miserable for both. Appropriate distance between the two depends on both speaker and listener conforming to circumstance and cultural expectations.

Intimate space:

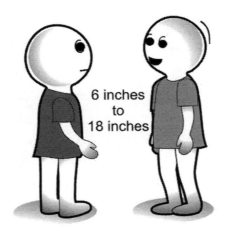

6 inches
to
18 inches

This is the area we regard as psychologically ours. This zone is reserved for a select group of people usually including family, love partners, and very close friends. If someone invades our intimate space, we often feel uncomfortable, angry, or anxious; and it's almost impossible to listen effectively because both brain and body are trying to restore a safe distance.

Personal space:

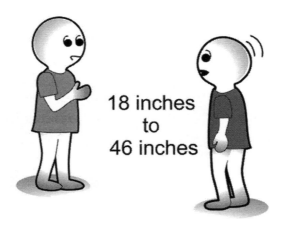

18 inches
to
46 inches

This is the amount of space we're comfortable with if we have a relationship with the people we're talking with. It's the distance we reserve for social gatherings such as parties and friendly interactions. If someone who doesn't belong is in our personal space, we can't listen effectively until we resolve the space issue.

Social space:

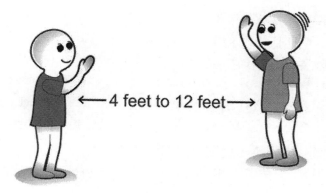

←— 4 feet to 12 feet —→

This is the distance we consider appropriate for business and formal social interactions, for acquaintances and for anyone with whom we don't have an established relationship.

Public space:

←over 12 feet→

Anything over 12 feet is typical in a public forum.

Each of these zones or spaces is normally the rule *within* our culture. However, in some situations people are accustomed to having their personal space encroached upon and have learned not to take offense or to stop listening to a person even when their normal personal zones have been violated, such as on a bus at rush-hour or at a crowded sporting event.

Listening effectively can become quite difficult when working with people of different cultures, whether on our home ground or theirs. But it is crucial that we understand the role distance plays so that we don't send the wrong signals with our actions.

Other cultures have different perspectives on what's considered acceptable as intimate, personal, and social space. We might find ourselves, for example, almost nose-to-nose in conversation with a Saudi Arabian business associate because what constitutes socially acceptable conversation space for him is considered intimate space in the United States. We would probably find ourselves backing away from him, trying to regain our social space, while the associate pursued us across the floor trying to maintain *his* customary distance.

Body language

There are a variety of ways body language can affect our listening, including being distracted or confused. If the speaker's body language seems to be at odds with what's being said, the mixed messages may leave us wondering which one we should believe. Distracting body language interferes with our listening ability because we can't concentrate on the message. On the other hand we may not even notice a speaker's body language, which can pose a different challenge to listening effectively. If we don't understand basic body language concepts and the effects they can have on us, we're less able to process what's truly being said, and we miss this added dimension to every message we listen to.

Body language is much more important than one might think. In fact, according to social psychologist Albert Mehrabian, PhD, research studies show that body language accounts for 55% of the overall message conveyed by a speaker.[3]

Knowing about and accurately processing the nonverbal signals we get from a speaker is essential to listening effectively. When we find ourselves confused as to the meaning of a speaker's message, we may have hit a body language barrier. Words seem to make sense, but something is not connecting. We are discomforted by an inconsistency that we cannot put our finger on, and we need to try to do something about it.

FOCUSED VIEW: POSSIBLE SOLUTIONS

If focused viewing is one of my specific listening issues, I could:

- Learn as much as I can about nonverbal language using videos, books, and articles.
- Observe people I know so I can see what their specific face and body language tell me.
- Apply the information and observations above to a set of people I do not know so I can become comfortable translating nonverbal language I see into usable information.

---

3   Albert Mehrabian, Nonverbal Communication (Independence, KY, Wadsworth Publishers, 1972).

Physically Affective Barriers

Physical Discomfort

Despite our best intentions, there are listening barriers due to physical conditions in the environment and in ourselves that make it difficult for us to listen effectively. We have a tendency to ignore these detrimental barriers to listening because we deal with them unconsciously all the time. It's important, however, to be conscious of these barriers because physical comfort is critical to being able to listen effectively. The four major physical barriers that can affect us are *temperature, uncomfortable seating, fatigue, and sensory overload.*

Temperature

Everyone is comfortable at different temperatures, and being too hot or cold can dramatically affect our ability to pay attention. If we're shivering, sweating, fanning ourselves, or rubbing our arms to stay warm, we're concentrating on trying to get comfortable. We're not listening. An uncomfortable physical environment poses a tremendous listening barrier.

Uncomfortable seating

The furniture we're sitting on can make a big difference in our ability to concentrate when we're seated while we're listening. Seating that's too hard, soft, low, high or in some other way uncomfortable puts a limit on our listening endurance. The old adage *"The mind can absorb only what the seat can endure"* holds true.

If sitting is uncomfortable, we're likely fidgeting or shifting to try to get comfortable. What we're not doing is listening. Shifting to find a comfortable position is an extremely distracting activity; and if we're trying to listen to someone while we're moving around, it's highly unlikely that we're paying attention to our speaker's message.

UNCOMFORTABLE SEATING: POSSIBLE SOLUTIONS
If uncomfortable seating is one of my listening barriers, I could:
- Keep a seat-sized pillow in the trunk to use when necessary.
- Call ahead to find out the meeting space's amenities.
- Find another chair or alternate being seated with standing in the back or side of the room.

Fatigue

We've all had the experience of "hitting the wall" and being unable to listen any more. Fatigue can be a matter of the time of day or the result of illness or lack of sleep. Whatever the cause, fatigue leads to low energy and low concentration, and it becomes difficult to listen effectively.

We know when our energy and ability to concentrate are at their highest, and we also know when our low points are throughout the day. Our ability to listen effectively follows the peaks and valleys of our energy levels. When we're so tired we can't concentrate and we realize we're not really absorbing anything that's being said, our mind shuts down. No matter how much we want to, we just can't participate effectively in the conversation.

FATIGUE: POSSIBLE SOLUTIONS

If fatigue is one of my listening barriers, I could:

• Know when my energy is at its lowest and avoid scheduling meetings at that time.

• Get a great night's sleep before important events or activities.

• Let the speakers know I'm too fatigued to give them the level of listening they deserve.

Sensory overload

When our senses are being bombarded by information, we're experiencing sensory overload. Any combination of visual, auditory, or discomfort-related barriers may create a sensory overload that lessens our ability to listen effectively. When we're confronted with multiple external listening barriers at once, we can't grasp the fullness of the message we're hearing; and the more stimuli we're faced with, the less effective our listening is. Our frustration, with a sense of being overwhelmed, becomes the listening barrier.

SENSORY OVERLOAD: POSSIBLE SOLUTIONS

If sensory overload is one of my listening barriers, I could:

- Get a great night's sleep before important events or activities take place.
- Let the speaker know I am too fatigued to give him or her the level of listening attention deserved.
- Dress in layered clothing to accommodate temperature variables.
- Bring a small pillow for long seminars.
- Sip water.
- Change positions every fifteen minutes to prevent soreness
- Speak up if I am tired or ill because such a condition will impair my listening.
- Avoid scheduling activities when my energy is usually at its lowest.
- Take a coffee, restroom, or other kind of break.

General Tools for External Barriers

Remove the Barrier

We must take responsibility for actively eliminating or minimizing the impact of external barriers that get in the way of our hearing, visual, and physical comfort. We can ask people in charge to adjust the temperature or respond to the fact that it's difficult to hear. We can ask people nearby to lower their voices, to stop tapping their pencil, or to generally refrain from activity that is distracting. Whether it's moving to be away from a distraction or just to avoid having to crane our necks to see the speaker, it's never rude for us to make it easier to concentrate and listen as long as we're courteous about it. Lastly, and this might be the most difficult, we can simply acknowledge a distraction, let it be, and try to ignore it. There's a reason someone coined the phrase "What is, *is!*"

Create A Listening Environment

When we're in charge of the listening environment ourselves, we can actively control the external barriers that might keep us from listening. We can moderate the room's temperature and arrange for comfortable seating, remove visual barriers, ask everyone to shut off their cell phones, and otherwise remove or minimize many environmental barriers to effective listening that we see. By preparing the listening environment in advance, we ensure more effective listening for ourselves and for everyone around us as well.

All of the measures we've been considering so far are intended to help us address the *external* listening barriers we might face, but these only represent one of the two principle barrier types there are. There's another type of obstruction that is just as capable of preventing us from listening effectively, *internal* barriers. Internal barriers can lurk within ourselves, distracting us from listening even though we don't realize it; and they can continue to be distracting until we take the time to see them for what they are.

CHAPTER THREE

INTERNAL LISTENING BARRIERS

EVERY ONE OF US HAS a different personal history and set of experiences that color how we think and react to people, situations, and the messages we listen to. We listen through a set of undetected filters gradually formed and put into place by us throughout our personal history. These barriers can distort the messages we receive or keep us from listening to them altogether.

There are seven major barriers that can spring up from *within ourselves*, ready to destroy the message being sent to us because they're in the way and we're not aware of them. These internal barriers that can inhibit our effective listening without our realizing it are:

judging and weighing   *hit-or-miss listening*
power and control   *language*
emotional triggers   *lack of focus*
performance anxiety

Each of these seven major barriers has within it a number of equally affective and identifiable sub-barriers that can hinder us also, and it is not at all unusual for some of them to apply to us while others do not.

Judging/Weighing Barriers

Whether we realize it or not, many times we judge what people say through a filter based either on how we feel about the person delivering the message or on its intent. We're not weighing the merit of the message based on its content. Instead, we're using our own built-in judgments and beliefs to downgrade or upgrade what is being said.

The major judging and weighing barriers include:

- Comparing
- Biased listening
- Interpretive filters
- Selective listening

First, we'll look at each barrier separately and follow it with some options for managing it. Finally, we'll look at all of these barriers as a group.

Comparing

It is a most human act to compare ourselves to the speakers we are listening to. We might compare ourselves to these messengers based on what we know about them, such as their educational level, their experience in the subject area, their reputation, or our own previous experience with them. This kind of barrier is based on how we think the speakers we listen to measure up to our preconceived ideas of what message they *should* be delivering and *how* they should be delivering it.

When we compare ourselves to a speaker in this way, we give greater or lesser significance to what we're listening to depending on our assessments; and in doing so, we don't give the message an impartial hearing. For example, we might expect a speaker who has a PhD to automatically have the upper hand in a conversation and a teenager to automatically have less to offer than we can.

One sign of this comparison barrier is self-talk. "Well, she has a PhD in sociology, so she must know" or "He's been a VP at US Bank for 10 years, so he must know all about..." Another one is verbalizing our comparison to others in conversation, either to praise or put down the speaker in light of our own expectations. "Well, I have my *master's* degree in that subject, and I feel..." or "After 20 years of being in retail, I found that..."

> "*At our family reunion a few years ago, I was in conversation with three other family members. It was a deep discussion about an ethical situation at one of our jobs dealing with the fact that management reduced payment of a deserved bonus. My then 13-year-old nephew, with his pants barely staying on his hips, came up to our group on his skateboard. I thought to myself, "What could he contribute of any value? He's a teenager and has no idea." When we all stopped talking, he proceeded to summarize what we said and then offered a pearl of wisdom. His comment? "The rule was in place when the sale happened, and even though the*

rule changed before the next paycheck, he's still owed the original, higher bonus. It's that simple."
That was the day I stopped considering age in my listening."

— Author

> ### COMPARING: POSSIBLE SOLUTIONS
> If comparing is one of my listening barriers, I could:
> - Be aware of when I start comparing myself to others.
> - Try to remember that everyone can have something of value to say.

Biased Listening

A WELL-KNOWN, OFT-TOLD, APOCRYPHAL STORY:

A gentleman went to a special seminar at Princeton University in the 1960s. When the speaker came onstage, his shirt was rumpled, his khakis had probably never seen an iron, and his hair was a mess. The man in the audience said to himself, "What the heck is this guy going to teach me?" The speaker opened his mouth and proceeded to mesmerize the audience with his brilliance and ability to make physics understandable. Who was it?

That speaker was Albert Einstein. This listener was weighing the speaker's worth based on appearance. Had he continued to judge the messenger according to his clothing bias, he might have discounted or lost most of the famous man's message!

Our life experience results in biases we may not be aware of. This barrier can color our listening in a way that distorts what we're listening to. We reshape the message being delivered by forming an opinion *in advance* about its value, such as basing the merits of the message on how we feel about the person or group we believe the speaker belongs to.

If we've never had a decent conversation with someone who is dressed like a stereotypical nerd, for example, we may be predisposed toward not listening effectively to people dressed that way. If someone speaks with an accent, we may summon up some bias of ours that keeps us from listening effectively. To be an effective listener, however, we need to get past this kind of limiting bias so we can capture the essence of the message. Part of what determines how effectively we listen depends on how open we are to the messenger.

Our ability to evaluate the content of a message can be easily compromised by any bias we've attached to the person speaking. We become blocked by internal dialogue with ourselves along the lines of "He couldn't possibly know what he's talking about" or "With an accent like that, what could she know?"

BIASED LISTENING: POSSIBLE SOLUTIONS

If biased listening is one of my listening barriers, I could:

- Make a list of specific biases I have toward people with whom I have come into contact, including recollections of when and how this bias came about. Then I could describe the emotion(s) I associate with each incident. If done honestly, I could unearth the reasons why this bias is getting in my way and discover the freedom it gives me to momentarily push it aside.

- Take note of how others are reacting to the speaker and consider whether I may be biased if others seem engaged while I am not.

Interpreting

Sometimes a spoken message can either be generally unclear or understood in more than one possible way. Each person listening interprets it differently. When a message does not have either a positive or negative slant to it that the speaker makes clear, we as listeners have a tendency to respond to its intent with our own attitudes, needs, and values based on our own experience. As the listener, we can only filter the information through our own history and experience.

A SHUTDOWN

A supervisor announced to the group that one of the manufacturing lines was being shut down next week. For one of the newer employees, that sentence creates fear because, in his old job, a line shutdown meant the beginning of the end of the company and his job. However, another worker's experience of a line shutdown meant that the machines were being retooled for a new product that made the company a considerable amount of money. Both men heard the same message, but interpreted it differently.

Because we listen to neutral or puzzling statements through our own filters, we attach our own positive or negative spin to the message. We recall the information through our own filter and cannot separate the effect of the filter from the content. As listeners, we might find it puzzling that others are evaluating the message differently and that there is disagreement as to what was really said. Others have not interpreted the language the same way we did. They might say to us, in later conversation, "That is not what the speaker said," or "Where did you get *that* idea from?"

> **INTERPRETING: POSSIBLE SOLUTIONS**
> If this is one of my specific listening issues, I could:
> • Watch the body language and emotions of others. If they are not responding as I am, a barrier might be present.

Selective Listening

When we listen only for information that interests us or helps prove us right in a discussion while we dismiss everything else, we're running into the selective listening barrier. Selective listening occurs when we mentally edit the message as it comes to us and pick out and listen only to the things that interest us, letting the other information slip past unnoticed.

A good example of selective listening is meeting someone new and hearing things about her hometown or her interesting hobbies, but later recalling only a few isolated facts, forgetting not only most of the conversation but even the person's name. Selective listening like this keeps us from taking in and recalling things we've heard. It even keeps us from being fully part of the conversation in the present.

We're unable to relate things we're hearing now to the things that were said earlier because we weren't listening to *everything* that was said. With selective listening, even if we take notes, we're still likely to get only parts of the message.

> **SELECTIVE LISTENING: POSSIBLE SOLUTIONS**
> If this is one of my specific listening issues, I could:
> * Begin each conversation with a commitment to listen to the complete message.
> * Repeat or rephrase information back to the speaker whenever possible to keep myself engaged in listening to the entire message.

Ways to Alleviate Our Judging/Weighing Barriers

Intent

Listen with an intent to learn from the speaker no matter what biases we may have. If we *listen to learn*, we may break the bias.

Practice

Sharpen the degree of listening with an openness. Instead of exercising judgment, enlist the cooperation of someone trustworthy and try out an exercise called *reversal*. Find a controversy that isn't too explosive and take turns having each person argue one side of the issue. Do it sincerely, and really push the argument each person is making. Don't stop until both participants feel immersed in arguing both sides reasonably.

Strategy

Alhough speaker-listener exchanges might not change a person's actual point of view, there's always something to be gained by listening carefully to opposing viewpoints.

Power and Control Barriers

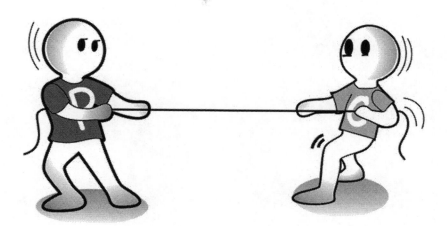

Power and control barriers arise when we persistently try to become the speaker ourselves rather than listening. Such behaviors may have deep roots coming from how we may have been treated by others in the past or from a currently irritating situation. Regardless of the source, power and control barriers can overpower our ability to listen effectively.

Power and control barriers include:

- Mind reading
- Identifying
- Interrupting
- Advising
- Sparring/ambushing
- Being right
- Speaker as a power figure
- Interconnecting with individuals/groups

Mind reading

Mind reading comes about when we, as listeners, *think* we know more about the message a speaker is trying to convey than he or she does. This barrier comes from making an assumption that the speaker is not clear about his or her message and we, through our powers of mental telepathy, have figured out what the message really *is* about and can clear everything up as soon as we open our mouth. We have become mind readers.

We stop listening while going through our own mental gymnastics, and we miss the fact that the speaker may have worked through the point in an entirely different way. We are devaluing the speaker and questioning the validity, importance, or significance of the message by assuming it will not be clear. We have put ourselves in a know-it-all position, a dangerous place for a listener to be. We are not only discounting or minimizing the message the speaker is trying to share with us before it has been fleshed out, but also disrespecting the speaker. While we are busy mentally preparing a helpful reply and saying to ourselves, "Where is he going with this?" or "I know what the problem really is" or "Let me help her get to the point," we are missing parts of the message.

> **MIND READING: POSSIBLE SOLUTIONS**
> If mind reading is one of my listening issues, I could:
> • Say to myself, "They are clear about the message they are sending. I'm here to listen and learn, not to teach or advise. I'm going to listen to the end."

Identifying

Have we ever heard someone tell a story and found ourselves wanting to interrupt? Do we switch the conversational focus back to ourselves by trying to come up with an equal or better story? Do we listen to the story primed for an "I can top that" moment? If we listen this way, we've hit an identifying barrier. What the speaker is saying reminds us of an experience, and we feel compelled to share it. Once it sounds as if we can relate *our* story, we listen only for a break in conversation so we can speak. Instead of participating in the experience the speaker wants to share with us, we've switched the focus to ourselves. We have left our speaker frustrated, unappreciated, and undervalued.

If a friend, for example, tells us about the car accident he was just in and we take over the conversation to tell about *our* car crash, we've stopped listening and decided to switch the conversational focus over to make *ourselves* the speaker. We're listening selectively for points we can identify with so we can take the floor away from the speaker. Our friend may never finish his story because he may have forgotten the point he was trying to make or sees no value in continuing with it. We've alienated and frustrated our friend with our own self-involvement.

Do we ever shift the conversational focus to ourselves by trying to come up with an equal or better story? Do we ever listen to people speaking just for an opportunity to take away the floor? Do we listen for "I can top that" opportunities? If we're guilty of any of these, *we* have become the barrier to effective listening!

IDENTIFYING: POSSIBLE SOLUTIONS

If identifying is one of my listening barriers, I could:

- Recount an experience only when and if it's appropriate and timely to introduce it.
- Make any of my intervening remarks short and in keeping with the speaker's message.
- Say something like, "When a similar thing happened to me, I wasn't as calm as you were" instead of telling my whole story.

Interrupting

The interrupting barrier becomes an obstruction when we cut the speaker off for the express purpose of taking control of the conversation. We feel compelled to speak and we don't want to listen. We interrupt in the middle of a sentence, not thinking about whether the interruption will contribute to the conversation or impede it.

By cutting speakers off, we don't allow them to deliver their entire message. We aren't showing them enough respect to let them finish. And though we may think we're interrupting for a good reason, what we say now is likely to be resented. Interrupted speakers feel that their message is being misunderstood, disrespected, or undervalued and may tune *us* out.

If we wonder if we're being an interrupter, there are some clues we can look for. Before we spoke, did we wait for the pause that let us know the speaker was done? Does the person we're talking to look frustrated? Are we drowning out the person currently speaking by barging in with speaking *our* words over his or hers?

Advising

The advising barrier is present when we stop listening to what the person is saying and instead search our memory banks for advice. In these situations, we become self-appointed problem-solvers. Our advice hasn't been requested but we're still listening with the intent of giving it. No matter who the person is or what the subject matter is, we're deciding about what advice we feel the speaker needs. If we're worried about whether or not we're acting as an advisor in conversation, we can ask ourselves, "Am I being actively receptive by listening or am I completely reactive by advising?"

ADVISING: POSSIBLE SOLUTIONS

If advising is one of my listening barriers, I could:

- Refrain from giving advice, reminding myself, "I am here to listen."
- When specifically asked for advice, say something relevant and in keeping with the request.
- Accept speaker gratitude graciously even though all I did was respond to what I was listening to.

Sparring

We're contending with the sparring barrier when our combative offense-defense mood interferes with our listening. In sparring, our main purpose in listening is to find things we disagree with. We have very strong opinions and positions and are dismissive of other people's points of view that don't agree with ours. We use sarcasm, put-downs, or remarks that are likely to change a discussion into an argument.

The sparring listener is waiting in ambush to pounce on the speaker (victim). If, for example, we are part of a baseball discussion and are listening only for an incorrect statistic we can take issue with, or are part of a discussion on movies and are listening only for an incorrect fact about who starred or what year the movie was made, we are sparring.

In sparring, we're focusing only on what the speaker has said that we think is wrong, and we cannot give fair hearing to other points the speaker has made during the entire message. Because we're constantly in attack mode, this kind of selective listening may result in a speaker who is unwilling or unable to engage in a conversation with us at all. When we constantly disagree with people on even the smallest of points, conversations become arguments that begin with tension and often end with bad feelings; and no one learns anything from them!

SPARRING: POSSIBLE SOLUTIONS

If sparring is one of my listening barriers, I could:

- Actively listen for the speaker's point of view and find places where I can agree on certain facts or concepts.
- Pretend I am in a debate and arguing on the same side as the speaker.

Being right

A need to be right in a conversation may be a remnant of a childhood adaptation to a family communication style where the parents modeled "being right" as the way to win a conversation. If we had a background like this, we would equate being right with our own self-image.

Because we're willing to go to any length to avoid being wrong, we put up a listening barrier. We can't listen to criticism, can't be corrected, and can't take suggestions for change. We may twist facts, raise our voices, become accusatory, and even call up the speaker's past errors to avoid being wrong.

Because of our need to be right, our mind shuts down as soon as differing opinions are offered; and we stop listening. Nothing sticks. We can't acknowledge or consider the fact that we might be wrong. Emotion takes over, and we stop being rational.

BEING RIGHT: POSSIBLE SOLUTIONS

If the need to be right is one of my listening barriers, I could:

- Accept the fact that I do not need to "win" a conversation.
- Pretend that I have a "beginner's mind" on the subject and treat the speaker as an expert who can increase my knowledge base.
- Use phrases that won't polarize or escalate the conversation, such as, "I'll think about that" or "What an interesting thought" or "I'm not sure I agree, but let me get back to you on that."

Speaker as power figure

When we feel uncomfortable in listening mode because we believe a speaker holds the power in a conversation, we're experiencing the speaker-as-power-figure barrier.

Deborah Borisoff, PhD, a professor at the Steinhardt School of Culture, Education, and Human Development, New York City, writes that Western society associates the act of speaking with "control and power" and the act of listening with "passivity."[4]

If we've bought into the notion that speaking represents control and power, then we also believe that listening connotes weakness and surrender, even though true power comes from our gathering of information through listening.

The speaker-as-power-figure barrier may be in play if we find ourselves thinking such things as, "She's had the floor too long. I need to say something" or "I haven't said anything, so he must think I have nothing to offer."

....
4   Deborah Borisoff, Listening in Everyday Life (Maryland: University Press of America, 1997).

> **SPEAKER AS POWER FIGURE: POSSIBLE SOLUTIONS**
> If the speaker as a power figure is one of my listening barriers, I could:
> - Think of my listening as "legal eavesdropping." Eavesdropping will make me feel as if I have just as much power as the speaker, and can accept or dismiss what I'm listening to at the same time.

Interconnecting with individual/groups

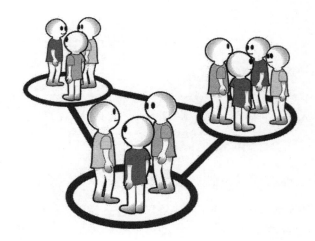

A network is made up of an informal interconnected group of entities, whether of individuals or organizations. In our personal, business, and professional lives we interact with these groups on a regular basis. We have a tendency to listen and respond differently to different people from different networks.

In business, there are bosses above, subordinates below, and colleagues on the same level. In our personal lives, we may have elders above, children below, siblings on the same level, and friends that inhabit different levels of importance. There are also people with whom we interact in special areas of interest, such as those involved in sports, hobbies, or school. We listen to all of them differently—bosses, subordinates, parents, siblings, best friends of 20 years, and new acquaintances.

To people in each of these networks we have attached a judgment on the *normal value* of our communication. Most of the time that value is based on our prior experience with them, their position in the network, and how recently they have become networked with us. As a result of the value we've given to these networks we may have also generated a barrier block that does not allow full listening to take place. Our internal dialogue may be, "She's only known me a few weeks, so her opinion can't be as valuable as my friend's opinion" or "He's from the other division, so he can't understand what we're doing."

Networks: Possible Solutions

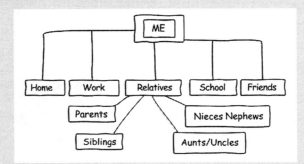

If the network barrier is one of my listening issues, I could:

- Map my personal networks by drawing a rectangle with "ME" inside. Draw a line from that rectangle, connecting it to other rectangles, each of which carries the name of one of my networks
- Once I have mapped my networks, I could look at each and honestly ask myself these questions in order to rate how effectively I listen to the people in them.
- Do I listen to old friends differently from new ones?
    - Do I listen to an administrative assistant differently from a person in authority?
    - Is any of this behavior hurting me?
    - How would listening effectively to all the people within my networks help me personally and professionally?

Emotional/Historical Trigger Barriers

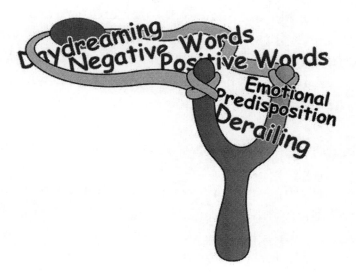

Emotional/historical trigger barriers can be the most difficult set of barriers to identify because they come from listening to a message through the filter of our own personal history. We may have been listening with these unconscious filters in place for so long that it's now second nature to have them in place. Because these barriers lie deep in internalized personal experience, it's difficult for us to diagnose them as barriers.

There are four emotional/historical triggers that can serve as major barriers to our effective listening:

- Emotional predisposition
- Daydreaming
- Positive words
- Negative words

Emotional Predisposition

If the speaker is saying something we *want* to hear, even if it is a half-truth or fiction, we open the door to our brain and allow everything to come through our listening capability without a reality filter in place. If, however, the message is something we do *not* want to hear about, we close the door to the unwanted, unpleasant, critical, or negative information. Our brain never receives it or considers its value. Because we don't want to listen to anything negative about our favorite coach, best boss, wonderful neighbor, or awesome coworker, for example, we slam the door and block the information as soon as we begin to hear negative information.

By closing doors to messages at will, we do not have to come to grips with viewpoints we disagree with. We close off our critical thinking and let our emotions evaluate what we're hearing. If our mind is filled either with emotionally positive words like "They are so right" or negative ones like "I don't want to hear this," we are in the midst of *emotional predisposition.*

> **EMOTIONAL PREDISPOSITION: POSSIBLE SOLUTIONS**
> If emotional predisposition is one of my listening barriers, I could:
> • Try to become instantly aware of instances where I am predisposed to the nature of the information coming in and make note of it.
> • Ask myself what it is that causes me to listen either with no filters in place, or so many filters in place that I shut my mind to information or open it with no reservation at all.

Daydreaming

When we suddenly find ourselves coming back into a conversation not knowing how the speaker got from where we left the conversation to where he or she is now, we are probably experiencing the daydreaming barrier. Something the speaker has said has triggered a chain reaction of our own personal memories, and now we've lost blocks of the speaker's conversation.

A daydreaming barrier can come up easily when we are fatigued or stressed because our ability to concentrate isn't at a high level. For example, if a coworker tells us about her trip to Disneyland with her family and we start remembering a memorable time twenty years ago when we enjoyed another recreational park, we have suspended listening for the moment in favor of revisiting our own memories.

Because we're busy imagining something else in thought, the speaker has become background noise to our stroll down memory lane. We are absorbing nothing new. When we finally catch ourselves coming back to the conversation later, we become well aware of the fact that we must have left it at some point in time and missed something.

> **DAYDREAMING: POSSIBLE SOLUTIONS**
> If daydreaming is one of my listening barriers, I could:
> • Realize I am no longer daydreaming, then attach my listening to what the speaker has just said to pull myself back into listening.

Positive Words

Words and phrases that evoke in us immediate, long-lasting, and positive emotional responses can interfere with continuing to listen. These words come from a personal history comprised of our childhood, teen, and adult experiences. Our high school English teacher, for instance, might have used the word "superb," "excellent," "wonderful," "awesome," when we did an excellent job on an assignment. Today, when our boss uses the same word "superb," we recall the positive emotion attached to that word twenty years ago, and we dwell on the word and bask in its glow. We're focusing now on the positive emotion attached to the use of a word or phrase by itself, not on the part it plays in a message. Because we respond so completely to the positive feelings we get, the delight becomes a barrier, and we miss what is said afterwards. While the speaker is still talking, we're congratulating ourselves. What we're not doing is listening.

Negative Words

When someone says something that hits us the wrong way because a specific word or phrase has been used, it may send us off the deep end and stop our listening immediately. This is the negative word barrier in action.

Just as positive words come from our life experience, negative words also come from a personal history comprising our childhood, teen, and adult life. These words can evoke an immediate, long-lasting, negative emotional response in us and interfere with our being able to keep listening effectively.

Negative words include all kinds of seemingly innocent words, ethnic slurs, sarcastic remarks, insults, and swear words that activate a listening barrier. Words such as "idiot," "unacceptable," "whatever," "bimbo," and "ugly" are just a few. If a speaker were to describe someone as a "cow" and we or someone close to us had been labeled that in the past, the emotion attached to that word would rise up and block our listening. As with positive words, negative words bring up emotions that can color everything we have heard and are still listening to. Our focus on our emotions blocks us from paying attention and we're no longer listening effectively. As we dwell on a particular word or phrase, we might say to ourselves, "I can't believe she said that!" or "I can't believe he went there. He's rude!" Our reaction to negative words tends to obstruct our listening effectiveness for as long as it takes us to get over the use of the word, a struggle during which we may miss important information.

> In fourth grade a fellow classmate told me I
> was ugly. At the age of nine I had no way of
> understanding jealousy, rivalries, or peer pressure.
> I just took what she told me as the truth.

I lived with that "truth" until the age of twenty-seven, when three wonderful friends worked with me to eliminate that thinking. It took a long time to undo the damage that the word "ugly" had caused.

Before I began doing some listening work on my own, when someone used the word "ugly," thoughts would go through my head of "Don't they know 'ugly' is on the inside not the outside?" or "Gosh, use the words 'homely' or 'plain.' Don't use 'ugly.' It's so mean.

Once I realized that "ugly" was one of the negative words that was stopping my listening, I began to work on minimizing the amount of time I was obsessing on the word and getting back to the conversation. Today, I am now able to push aside those thoughts within a second or two.

— Chris

Ways to Alleviate Emotional/Historical Triggers

One of the best ways for us to make emotional/historical words or situations or perceptions no longer block our listening is to identify them and understand why they evoke certain emotions in us. In order to do this, indentifying the source of these three types of emotional/historical barrier should help: the situational occurence, the forbidden topic, and the effect of word choice.

The situational occurence

Situational circumstances can create difficult episodes in our lives that we can't forget. This can be anything from having broken a violin string during a grade school performance to missing the winning basket in a varsity basketball game to losing a job.

The forbidden topic

Forbidden topics are those we will not talk about. There's nothing wrong with having topics forbidden as long as we know why. Being a responsible listener also means being responsible for our emotional needs when a topic is out of bounds for us. We can make our apologies and leave the conversation. We don't have to just sit through it.

The effects of word choice

As discussed earlier, specific words can trigger a response in us. No matter when or where we hear them, they can stop our listening. Creating a list of our trigger words will heighten our awareness of them so we can push them aside momentarily. When we can no longer push the words aside momentarily, we must consider removing ourselves from the conversation in order to take care of our own emotional needs.

Here is a strictly personal exercise for you to consider:

....

A Strictly Personal Exercise

Instructions

[Before you begin filling out the columns of the form you create for this exercise, make a copy for future use by yourself or others.]

Create three verticle columns on an empty page.
In column 1: Word/Topic/Situation

Write down the most problematic words, phrases, situations, or topics that stir up emotions that are negative enough to stop you from listening.

In column 2: When and How

Once you identify the triggers, write down when and how they became so emotionally loaded.

In column 3: Age at First Occurrence

Identify the age when this trigger first became an issue.

Example:

(1) Word – *ugly*

(2) When and How – *I was called this in fourth grade, never said anything to my parents about it, and internalized it.*

(3) Age - *10*

Example:

(1) Word – *unacceptable*

(2) When and How - *the VP of a company that I was a district manager for said this continuously and with uncalled-for venom.*

(3) Age – *46*

....

Those of us who engaged in this personal exercise now have a good idea about where many of our barrier words, topics, and situations came from and why they're an issue for us. We also know when these circumstances, topics, or words first became a problem.

If we participated in the exercise we have a choice now. Whenever those triggers come up, we can choose to become emotionally engaged *at the age we were when it became an issue* or we can say to ourselves, "That's one of my emotional triggers. I'll get back to listening and talk to the person about it later." We can either continue to avoid listening or start contributing to the conversation.

Remember, the speaker is not a mind reader and has no idea that a word or topic has touched us favorably or unfavorably. Listening becomes *our* choice because we are aware of how certain words or topics affect us.

Performance Anxiety Barriers

Performance anxiety barriers are barriers that usually come up in stressful situations, such as meeting new people, making a first impression, being interviewed, or taking part in a meeting. We tend to have two major performance anxiety barriers:

- Rehearsing
- Intruding

Rehearsing

The first sign of the rehearsing barrier shows up when we've turned our listening off right after the speaker makes a point we want to respond to. What the speaker is saying has become background noise. We find ourselves rehearsing internally what we're going to say even though we're in the middle of a conversation.

This rehearsing barrier comes from our own insecurity. We may believe that if we do not rehearse, our upcoming response will be judged negatively. We're constantly thinking about what we're going to say while the other person is talking. We have an ongoing preoccupation with our own performance or image while the conversation is taking place.

This kind of performance anxiety can happen particularly when we are among people we don't know or with whom we're not comfortable. The occasion dulls our listening capability because we can't rehearse and listen at the same time. While we spend our time preparing our next comment, not only do we lose the flow of what's being said, but we risk either repeating something that has already been said or responding in some other inappropriate way.

PERFORMANCE ANXIETY: POSSIBLE SOLUTIONS
If performance anxiety is one of my listening barriers, I could:
- Prepare for those conversations where thinking about the matter in advance will benefit me. With research and notes in hand or solidly in my mind, my main points and backup research will be available. I can listen to the thread of the discussion without needing to rehearse.
- Prepare for the people I know will be there. What might they think about the subject? How do they respond to the way information or questioning is phrased? What are their hot buttons?

Intruding

The intruding barrier is different from the interrupting barrier that we considered earlier when we looked at power and control situations we might find ourselves in. We don't intrude out of a need for control; we intrude solely out of fear of forgetting what we want to say. We have that "flash of insight" that we're afraid will disappear unless we voice our thought at once. We're concentrating on our anxiety about our own message instead of listening to the one that's being delivered. Because we're worried about forgetting what we're going to say, we focus on thinking about our reply and stop listening effectively to the conversation at hand.

INTRUDING: POSSIBLE SOLUTIONS

If intruding is one of my specific listening issues, I could:

- Attach a keyword to a response I want to make so that I can remember it. Jot it down if at all possible, so I don't forget the idea. When it's proper to become a speaker, my keyword will bring back my idea.
- I won't write complete sentences, just key phrases or the words the speaker used that provoked me to want to introduce my own thoughts. I'll count on having a tiny notepad in my jacket, purse, and car just for this purpose.

Hit-or-Miss Listening Barriers

Hit-or-miss listening barriers can surface when we don't put deliberate energy into listening effectively. Either we are expending only enough energy to *hear* rather than to *listen* or we're listening selectively. Our major hit-or-miss barriers include:

- Placating
- Hearing the expected
- Law of least effort
- Fact finding
- Listening for emotion

Placating

We're placating when we pretend to listen to the speaker and want the speaker to *think* we're listening while we're thinking about other things. We may engage in excessive eye contact, body language changes, or nods and smiles that don't match what's being discussed because we're not really listening to what the speaker is saying. We may be placating because we're tired, bored, or not interested in the speaker's subject. We're trying so hard to pretend that we're listening that we don't have the energy left to really listen. Our focus is on appearing to show interest rather than on listening effectively to the message.

> **PLACATING: POSSIBLE SOLUTIONS**
> If placating is one of my listening barriers, I could:
> - Check my thoughts and body language for signs of not being engaged.

Hearing the Expected

When we finish someone's sentence in our head with what we *expect* to hear instead of actually listening for how the speaker ends the sentence, we're dealing with the hearing-the-expected barrier. Because of prior interactions with that person on a particular subject, we fail to hear what is actually being said. If Joe, for instance, is always talking about how unfair his coach has been; and if in his next conversation with us he begins with "My coach...," we finish his unfinished sentence in our mind and mentally wander off. Because we've already completed what we predict the speaker's message will be, we miss Joe saying, "My coach told me how much I've improved this month."

When we assume the speaker will say the same old thing or have the same old attitude about a topic, we dismiss what is being said and predict the message content. If we manage to wander back into the conversation and find that the speaker isn't saying what we expected to hear, the hearing-the-expected barrier has made us miss something.

> **HEARING THE EXPECTED: POSSIBLE SOLUTIONS**
> If hearing the expected is one of my listening barriers, I could:
> * Approach each listening situation without regard to any previous history about the speaker but as a new experience.

Law of Least Effort

When we as listeners choose to listen to messages that call for the least effort to interpret and avoid those that are more complex in nature, we're under the influence of a barrier called the *law of least effort*. If two doctors were to examine us, for instance, and one explained our problem and treatment with Latin medical terms and complicated directions while the other explained things in laymen's terms in a logical order, we would be more likely to listen to the less complex explanation. Even though we were given essentially the same information, less effort would be required to understand the second doctor's message.

Advertising firms in the United States often make a point of presenting and directing their material to many prospective buyers at sixth-grade level, not because the average educational level of their target audience is that low but because the level of their listening skills is low. If we ourselves always listen to simple messages requiring the least amount of effort when given a choice, we could lose our ability to listen effectively to messages that are more complex. We could miss out on important nuances and find ourselves either struggling to understand what we're hearing or just giving up trying.

> **LAW OF LEAST EFFORT: POSSIBLE SOLUTIONS**
> If the law of least effort is one of my listening barriers, I could:
> • Approach each listening situation as a learning opportunity that requires me to put all of my listening skills to work.

Fact Finding

When we listen only for the facts, we don't get the full message that's being sent. Imagine, for example, a policeman interviewing a suspect and listening only to the facts and not the underlying emotional content. He will not get the complete story that is necessary in order to accurately report his overall assessment of the case.

By dismissing the overtones and undertones in the emotions or behaviors we catch from the speaker, we get only part of the story.

The role body language plays has been forgotten, and we are not listening effectively.

> **FACT FINDING: POSSIBLE SOLUTIONS**
> If fact finding is one of my listening barriers, I could:
> • Look for and take in additional messages I'm getting from the emotions and behaviors intertwined with these facts.

Listening for Emotion

When we listen *only* for the emotions that underlie a message, we miss the full content of the message. We get to know how speakers feel but not why they feel that way. Our sole intent is to be emotionally supportive. We might, for example, have a first conversation with a friend since she was laid off her job and concentrate on her emotional state to the exclusion of listening for the facts about the layoff. In concentrating just on the feelings of the speaker, we would miss the underlying reasons beneath the feelings; and because we didn't get the full message, we couldn't process and respond satisfactorily. We're either finding ourselves baffled as to why the person we've been talking to is upset or just not listening fully enough because we're waiting to console this devastated person.

> **LISTENING FOR EMOTION: POSSIBLE SOLUTIONS**
> If listening for emotion is one of my listening barriers, I could:
> • Try to find out as many facts as possible about what's causing the speaker's emotion in order to add my offer of support.

Ways to Alleviate Hit-or-Miss Barriers

Practice

Listen for the total message in situations we're not directly a part of whether the speaker is talking in a live situation or on a television, radio, or other type of broadcast. If necessary, we can take notes to ensure we are processing *both* factual and emotional content.

Imagine

Picture ourselves as a thirsty sponge. Imagine that we're drinking in everything: facts, emotions, body language, and behavior. We'll squeeze out what we don't want afterwards. This way we'll take in everything that was said, and do our filtering later, after the conversation.

Listen in reverse purposely

If we normally listen for emotion, listen for facts, and vice versa. If we normally listen for facts, look for emotional cues. Note how listening for both fact and emotion rounds out our understanding of the message and the messenger.

Language Barriers

Could most of us, as United States residents, understand what was meant if we heard someone use one of these phrases?

"Set a pick"	**"Pumpkin positive"**	**"Red light fever"**
Basketball Term	*Medical Term*	*Broadcasting Term*
The strategy of positioning oneself so a teammate can get away from the person covering him	Slang for lacking in intelligence	Fear about the quality of one's on-camera performance

A word is a unique unit of language consisting of one or more spoken sounds or their written representation. Words function as principal carriers of meaning. They can mean different things to different people because we filter words through our own beliefs, knowledge, upbringing, and experience with them. No two people are likely to attach exactly the same meaning to the same word or expression.

Language barriers arise when we don't understand something and we don't ask speakers to clarify or give us some form of explanation. We can't know every piece of history, every literary reference, or every word spoken in the world, so we should not hesitate to ask when something is unfamiliar.

Our major language barriers include:

- Idioms
- Metaphor
- Known and unknown cultures
- Vocabulary level

> *"In the ten years I've been facilitating listening seminars for all types of organizations, there is one job group that consistently has language as their top barrier, professors, teachers, trainers, and facilitators. What became apparent to me through my questioning them about this is the uneasy feeling they get when they "should know" all the words participants use. They're reluctant to reveal that they don't know*

a word or a phrase. As a result, they tend to stop
listening in order to try to figure out its meaning
through the context in which it has been used."

— Author

Idioms

Idioms are distinctive words and phrases in the usage of a language that are understood by people who are part of a particular group. They have a meaning that outsider's can't grasp because they are not members of that group. They can often depart from the literal meaning of their individual words. When we listen to such idiomatic expressions, our lack of knowledge of these idioms can become barriers to our understanding the message.

We expect to evaluate words we hear through the language filters we've acquired as we developed our language skills; but, depending on the part of the country we've lived in, we might expect to hear either "sack" or "bag" to describe the storage container we put our groceries in, or "water fountain" or "bubbler" to describe the machine we drink water from in a public place. Here are a few more idioms in which the use of each word in the phrase does not make sense to an outsider unfamiliar with them when put together in a phrase:

Head over heels	Off the hook
High on the hog	Method to my madness
Jump the gun	Pass the buck
Like a chicken with its head cut off	Saved by the bell

If the idiom as it's being used doesn't seem to fit what we either know or understand the individual words to mean, we recognize that the speaker likely means something very different. If we focus on trying to figure out the speaker's meaning, we may end up missing the rest of the message. If we have a chance to ask for clarification, it will allow us to go back to listening effectively.

> **IDIOMS: POSSIBLE SOLUTIONS**
> If this is one of my specific listening issues, I could:
> • Ask the speaker for a rephrase.
> • Research the phrase later to understand its meaning.

Metaphor

Metaphor is a language technique used to explain something by comparing the charateristics of one item to another item. If we don't understand the comparison, we stop listening while trying to figure out what the speaker's saying; and the metaphor becomes a barrier.

If someone says, for example, "My father is the duct tape that holds our family together," the expression contains two entirely different things that have been put together, father and duct tape. The metaphor has been based on the physical characteristics of *duct tape and the interpersonal characteristics of a father.* It tells the listener that father is a person who makes sure the family sticks together.

All cultures have words and phrases they can use metaphorically to put two entirely different things together in a special context which means something to their listeners because they are familiar enough with the language of that particular group. They can be expressions coming often from nature, war, sports, time, food, animals, and other areas that have sprung up from their shared history. When we as listeners don't "get" the metaphor, what was intended to enlighten us or communicate to us just becomes confusing. Both speaker and listener are not sharing the same everyday language, and it becomes a barrier not easily overcome. While we're trying to understand the speaker's metaphor, we're missing a part of the message. We're thinking, "I understand the words, but I don't get the meaning." We're totally confused about what the speaker is trying to say.

> **METAPHOR: POSSIBLE SOLUTIONS**
> If metaphor is one of my specific listening issues, I could:
> • Ask for a rephrase.
> • Write the phrase down so I can get back to listening and look it up later.
> • Get back to listening in case the meaning of the word becomes clear because of what the speaker says next.

Known and Unknown Cultures

A culture can be geographically based; it can be based on shared traditions, history, cuisine and folklore; it can be based on socioeconomic class; it can be based on educational level; it can be based on generations; and it can be based on an organization's shared values and behaviors.

When speakers naturally refer to what they consider public knowledge and we don't understand the basic terms common to their culture's geography, science, history, civics, beliefs, sports, or literature, many conversations can become hard for us to follow; and the speaker's references then can easily become barriers. For this reason, the degree to which we are culturally literate will affect the degree to which we can listen effectively.

For example, if a speaker said to us, "What the game of baseball needs now is someone like Joe DiMaggio," only those of us who knew that Joe was both a gentleman and a legendary baseball player would understand the point the speaker was making. In this case, cultural literacy would depend on how many generations back one's knowledge of sports in the United States reached.

Differences in educational exposure alone can have a huge impact on the breadth of cultural literacy. Novels taught in New England's elementary and high schools can be different from those in the Mid-Atlantic, the South, the Heartland, and the West. The same is true of textbooks used for history and the social sciences. We cannot expect to always have the same knowledge base as the speaker.

Whenever we realize that we do not understand a message because of the cultural references being made within it, we know that a listening barrier has popped up. Our self-talk may be "Why does he have to make points with stuff I don't understand?" or "What the heck does that phrase mean?" Because we are losing vital parts of the message, we may begin to tune out.

KNOWN AND UNKNOWN CULTURES: POSSIBLE SOLUTIONS

If cultural literacy is one of my listening barriers, I could:

- Ask for clarification.
- Research regional phrases.
- Use a cultural literacy dictionary
- Get back to listening, in case the meaning of the cultural reference becomes clear in what the speaker says next.

Vocabulary

When the words a speaker uses are not in our vocabulary, our lack of knowledge about the word becomes a barrier. If we cannot understand a word in the context of a sentence, we cannot totally understand the message. We then spend time trying to figure out the meaning of the word, missing the message as a whole because we cannot capture parts of it. We think to ourselves, "I wish they would use simple words I'm familiar with." We sense that we're getting stuck on a word, and we can't let go of the fact that we don't know exactly what it means.

How can we know it all?

Attenuate	Blandishment	Caprice	Clandestine
Desiccate	Eclectic	Encomium	Exculpate
Iconoclast	Inchoate	Misogynist	Obdurate
Peccadillo	Pusillanimous	Savant	Sedulous
Turpitude	Zealot		

VOCABULARY: POSSIBLE SOLUTIONS
If vocabulary is one of my listening barriers, I could:
- Ask for clarification if possible.
- Write the word down as close to the spelling I imagine and look it up for later clarification.
- Get back to listening, in case the meaning of the word becomes clear through what the speaker says next.

Alleviating Language Barriers

Ask for clarification

Do not fail to ask for clarification for fear of being thought uneducated. We will be heroes to anyone in the room who is confused too. Others in the room may rejoice because we had the courage to ask.

- It is easy to ask for clarification without feeling diminished if we have a few stock questions ready. We can say, "I'm sorry. Could you rephrase that?" or "I'm not clear as to how you are using that metaphor. Could you explain?"
- We can put the ball back in the speaker's court and call for a rephrasing that is more understandable. The speaker does not have to know why it is unclear to us. The speaker wants to be understood and will therefore rephrase the message. Once we get the clarification, we will not only understand the message but also learn a new word, metaphor, concept, or cultural reference at the same time!

Jot down a note

When at a lecture or seminar where we cannot ask the speaker to rephrase, we can write down the unclear word, metaphor, or reference so that we can get clarification immediately after the session ends. We can look up anything we do not understand, whether it showed up in conversation, on the radio or television, or elsewhere. Make a note of it and *look it up*. It is likely that the topic, word, or phrase will come up again.

Lack of Focus Barrier

Despite our best intentions, the lack of focus barrier can make listening difficult at any time, either because of an At-Birth barrier we all have begun life with or a Preoccupation with Other Issues barrier that life's complexity refuses to let us ignore.

The At-Birth Barrier

Thanks to Professor Wolvin's research at the University of Maryland, we know that people speak at 100 to 175 words per minute (WPM). Because we can listen intelligently to 600 to 800 words per minute (WPM), the gap between the high number of words we are capable of listening to and the much lower speed at which a speaker can talk to us makes it easy for us to wander and lose focus. As a result, we mistakenly believe we can deal with other things while listening to the person speaking to us.

Preoccupation with Other Issues Barrier

We have hit the Preoccupation barrier when we focus on matters that are outside of the conversation at hand. We may be thinking about what people are wearing, what we are going to buy at the supermarket, how we are going to get a raise, or how to solve a demanding personal problem. Our preoccupation leads us to place the current conversation, although somewhat important to us, much lower in priority than those other issues. Our mind wanders, and we lose both the substance and emotional content of the speaker's message. When we lose spontaneity and meaningful interaction because we are having an entirely separate conversation with ourselves about our current preoccupation, we weaken our ability to listen effectively.

> **LACK OF FOCUS: POSSIBLE SOLUTIONS**
> If lack of focus is one of my specific listening issues, I could:
> - Refocus. Change the self-talk that is coming out of my preoccupation with another issue to, "I'm not listening anymore. I need to get back to listening."
> - Remember current limitations. Tell myself that the other matters cluttering up my mind cannot be resolved right now anyway. Listening to what is going on is a better idea.

CHAPTER FOUR

APPLYING OUR KNOWLEDGE OF BARRIERS TO OUR OWN LIVES

WE'VE BEEN READING and thinking about the ways in which external and internal barriers can hinder our ability to listen effectively. If we internalize what we've learned about the barriers specific to us, we can use that knowledge to enrich our self-esteem, our relationships, and our communication with others. Now is the time to apply our awareness in a concrete way. Some self-management tools can help us take advantage of what we've learned.

General Self-Management Tools

Turning new knowledge into self-management tools allows us to push aside our personal listening barriers whenever we choose to do so. Rarely will we be able to erase them entirely because years of their being in place have given them a life of their own. But now, because we're becoming aware of them, we should be able to alleviate the effect they have on us.

Take Responsibility for My Listening

It is *our* responsibility, not the speaker's, to make sure that our listening needs are being met so we can listen effectively. As with any other skill, it is up to us to improve in any way we can. It helps to remember that the speaker can't read minds and doesn't know that a specific word might be one of our negative words or that a metaphor might have left us puzzled. Speakers don't know whether or not we're hearing them clearly. Neither do they know if we're preoccupied with other thoughts. Only *we* know what is going on in our brain. The responsibility for our listening rests with us.

Taking responsibility means asking questions when we don't understand what someone is saying. If body language doesn't agree with the spoken words, we're the ones obliged to ask speakers to clear up the discrepancy. When physical issues are present that might affect our listening, we're the ones who must be willing to speak up if conditions can be changed. Being responsible means asking for the music volume to be lowered or the door to be closed. We may even need to excuse ourselves from a conversation rather than pretend to be listening when the subject is one we can't handle. Taking responsibility also means acknowledging speakers favorably in a way that inspires them to continue.

Choose to Listen

Our motivation to listen affects whether we will push aside barriers. Why are we listening? Are we listening because we really want to be in the conversation or meeting? Because we respect the person talking? To give advice? To learn? We're not going to be effective listeners if we can't decide why we're listening.

When we actively choose to do our best at sports, music, or learning a new subject, our choice produces positive results. The same is true of listening. When we choose to commit ourselves to the process of listening, the degree of our commitment determines our effectiveness as a listener.

Listen to My Internal Dialogue

Every time we stop for an internal dialogue, whether we're listening to what our "self" is saying to us or how we're going to respond to a speaker, we're listening to and reflecting upon our own mind chatter. We're increasing our self-awareness of why we're reacting the way we are. In listening to ourselves, we're able to identify barriers that are coloring our interpretation and recognize them for what they are. Remember though, we don't want to be in this internal dialogue for long, because it takes us away from listening.

Stop Talking!

Listening means that we take in what the speaker is saying. To do this, we need to stop talking! As difficult as it may be sometimes, *not* talking can move a conversation forward because the speaker gets a chance to fully develop and complete a thought. It's amazing how much we can learn about people's lives, what motivates them, what they know, and what they're passionate about if we just listen. Bernard M. Baruch, adviser to six presidents writes, "Most of the successful people I've known are the ones who do more listening than talking."

Be Comfortable with Silence

Sometimes in conversation, silence just happens. When both speaker and listener are listening effectively, there can be silence while each formulates a response to what has just been said. We need to be comfortable with silence like this because taking that time allows our responses to be thoughtful and on target. Because people can be uncomfortable with silence, we might consider giving a little feedback, such as an earnest look or a simple nod of the head. But be assured that even if our silence leads to an uncomfortable pause, our conversation partner will be pleased to receive a thoughtful response from us, one that shows we were really paying attention.

Keep Eye Contact

Focusing our eyes on the speaker tells the speaker that we're listening. When we keep our eyes only on the speaker, it helps remove other visual distractions and allows our peripheral vision to examine whether the speaker's body language is saying something different from the words being used. Staring directly into someone's eyes might be very difficult for us to maintain; but looking at a speaker's whole face is an easy way to maintain eye contact in a natural manner.

Watch Body Language

Pay attention to what the speaker's body language is conveying. If we watch for positive and negative body language, we can become aware of how and why we're reacting to a speaker. Our job is to concentrate on the subject at hand in order to listen to the speaker's message effectively.

Give Feedback

We have three ways to give a speaker feedback: non-word utterances; body language; and questions for clarification. This kind of feedback does not intrude. It tells the speaker we're listening, and it helps maintain our concentration.

Nonword utterances

Using responses like "uh-huh," "ah," and "hmm" while a speaker is talking keeps us concentrating on the message and tells the speaker that the message is getting across.

Body language

A receptive posture conveys a receptive mind. Leaning forward with head forward, arms uncrossed, and an erect posture engages us and encourages the speaker. Making conscious choices about body language keeps us concentrating on listening.

Questions for clarification

Being willing and ready to ask questions when we need an explanation keeps our concentration at a high level. Asking questions, rather than relying on what we thought was said, also ensures our understanding of the message we're receiving.

Rephrase Content and Emotion

Taking time to condense and rephrase the message's content and the emotion behind it helps us to confirm what we've received and to compare it with what the speaker appears to have intended. Misconceptions can be cleared up immediately.

Role Play

If someone we trust can role-play with us, we can recreate each of our major barriers. Together we can use words or situations that bring a barrier to life and role-play interior dialogue and body language that helps us push aside the barrier. With role-playing, we become confident that we can lessen the impact of a barrier. We can listen more intently and effectively than we might have done had we not overcome the challenge of the barrier.

Write It Down

When we encounter a barrier, we need to write down what circumstances made the barrier surface for us. What kind of situation triggers a certain barrier? Once we jot down the specifics of an incident, including both the facts and emotions involved, we can take time to delve into our past in order to understand where the barrier came from. We must not willfully censor! Instead, we should be kind in our recollections but honest. Writing these occasions down will strengthen our listening skills, our communication skills, and our life.

Be Aware of the Listening Environment

Whenever we're called upon to listen, we're always subject to the physical conditions that exist in the environment that surround us at the moment. How we adjust to those conditions determines the extent to which we're able to listen effectively. Although we've considered the following situations earlier, here are a few major situations we've discussed that are well worth recognizing. They come with a bunch of do's and don'ts.

- Do not try to handle two different activities of any kind at the same time.
- Sit diagonally or across from the person(s) speaking to allow for eye contact and to avoid distractions.
- Keep status issues from arising. Unless the speaker is formally in front of an audience, either everyone in the conversation stands or everyone sits. All those in a conversation should be on the same level.
- Find a place away from distractions when sharing a conversation with a significant other and/or children.
- If it is not a good time to listen to someone who has approached us, we must say so! We then owe that person a time when we *can* listen. Make sure that time is kept!
- Be aware of others' energy. If people are anxious to talk, let them talk.

Find a Way to Be Interested in the Subject

In every conversation, lecture, seminar, or speech, there is likely to be something of interest to us. When the subject changes to something we're not interested in, we should rejoice! We now have the opportunity to learn something new that we can use later on.

Suspend Self

We need to do everything in our power to take the "I" out of listening. M. Scott Peck, MD, a nationally recognized author and lecturer in psychology, has stated that "an essential part of true listening is the discipline of temporarily giving up or setting aside one's own prejudices, frames of reference, and desires so as to experience, as far as possible, the speaker's world from inside his or her shoes."[5]

When we suspend self as the listener, we are able to truly take in the speaker's message without filtering the content and emotion we receive through our own listening barriers.

SELF-MANAGEMENT TOOLS

If self-management tools are the answer to Listen to Succeed triumphs, I could remember these Fourteen Catchphrases. If I put them into my memory bank, I can put every one of these strategies into play whenever and wherever I need to:

- Take responsibility for my listening
- Choose to listen
- Listen to my internal dialogue
- Stop talking!
- Be comfortable with silence
- Keep eye contact
- Watch body language
- Give feedback
- Rephrase content and emotion
- Role play
- Write it down
- Be aware of the listening environment
- Find a way to be interested in the subject
- Suspend self

I'm wishing myself good luck!

---

5   M. Scott Peck, The Road Less Travelled (New York: Simon and Schuster, 1978).

Focused Strategies for Enhanced Listening

Not only can we improve our own listening, but we can also use strategies to help others have more productive listening experiences too. Whether at home or at work, with friends or with people we have just met, applying the three practices which follow can enhance everyone's listening experience.

An Environment for Listening

Interruptions in conversations are disruptive to both the speaker and the listener. They are often unintentionally disrespectful. Everything from e-mail chimes to cell phone rings to other people stepping into a conversation already in progress interrupts the listening process. If we can do so, it is our job to eliminate these interruptions as best we can. Every step we take to show we are focused on everyone's listening needs shows the participants our respect for them. It also allows *us* to be effective listeners.

Here is a sample of a setup routine for business meetings that maximizes opportunities for effective listening:

- Arrange seating in as circular a setup as possible. It maximizes eye contact and makes all participants feel that everyone's input is valuable.
- Have a white board or flip chart labeled "General Purpose Parking Lot" already set up in the room. The General Purpose Parking Lot is the place where comments and concerns that might take the meeting off track can be written down. All participants should be aware that "parking lot" comments will be dealt with at the end of the meeting. As a result, everyone will get back to listening to what's currently under discussion.
- Use an "In Session" or "Stop" sign on the outside of the door when a conversation should not be disturbed. Although we may have to train outsiders to respect the sign, assure them that we will be available to speak with them when the sign comes down.
- Have as many seats at the table as the number of people expected. Remove extra seats whenever possible in order to create a more personal atmosphere.
- Be ready to ask participants to turn off cell phones or put them on vibrate.

A "Personal Parking Lot"

Having a Personal Parking Lot is a strategic maneuver for keeping conversations "on track." It's a *parking place on paper* where we can temporarily dump our thoughts so they will not stand in the way of our listening. We have not repressed our thoughts or decided to throw them out. We have only acknowledged the fact that spending time on them is not right or necessary at the moment. The great benefit of having a personal parking lot is that our thoughts will still be parked should we need them.

Our ever-ready, small notebook becomes our parking lot. It allows us to write down a few key words now and then that a speaker mentions that we want to respond to. Having them on hand will trigger any questions or comments we wanted to bring up later.

Create a Listening Plan

Listening effectively is a skill that we can always get better at through knowledge, reflection, and practice. All of the concepts and information we've considered in this book are ready and waiting for us to take advantage of; and they'll have a greater impact on our lives if we create a plan for action that combines all the pieces and puts each of them into practice. The more specific our plan, the better the results.

At minimum, our plan for better listening needs to include:

- Letting others know that we're working to enhance our listening.
- Asking someone in our life whom we consider to be an excellent listener to be our mentor in the area of listening.
- Identifying and asking certain people in our life to observe us as both a listener and a speaker, expecting them to give us their honest feedback about what they see and hear.
- Observing others while they are in listening mode to see what their behavior can teach us.

AFTERWORD

I close this book with the words I wrote at the beginning of it, a tribute to my grandmother's wisdom. "Listen without judgment," she said, "and wait for the period at the end of the sentence before formulating a reply." It is the foundation upon which *Listen to Succeed* has been written.

I invite my readers to benefit from her wisdom and to begin enjoying the fruits of enhanced listening in their own lives. Although I was lucky to have parents and a grandmother who were selfless listeners, I know how rare that can be.

My hope is that all my readers will take their understanding of both the importance of effective listening and the listening barriers that confront us in order to develop a new listening plan tailored specifically for themselves, one which will carry their personal and professional lives successfully into the future.

LISTENING EFFECTIVENESS PROFILE

Now that you've learned about the barriers that can impede your effective listening, you can discover exactly which barriers are the most problematic for you in your own life.

The Listening Effectiveness Profile©, in use since 2001, is an instrument designed to measure to what extent external factors and internal factors are playing a significant part in your own personal and professional life.

By questioning you about a number of your own attitudes and habits when you are engaging in an array of listening activities, The Listening Effectiveness Profile© instrument allows you to arrive at an objective, private assessment of where your strengths and weaker abilities lie when listening to the messages you receive from those with whom you're speaking. Once you see your Private Assessment Results, you will have given yourself a broad, honest, and wholly personal view of how adept you are at listening effectively.

To engage in your own personal Listening Effectiveness Profile© instrument and receive the accompanying Assessment Results, you can contact Listen to Succeed, LLC, at www.listentosucceed.com in order to acquire the necessary material.

ABOUT THE AUTHOR

Leslie Shore, M.A., is the owner of *Listen to Succeed*, a consultancy that focuses on using listening analytics to help personal and professional clients achieve their highest level of effective communication. Her work with corporations, nonprofits, entrepreneurs, health professionals, and educational institutions in the development of intra-personal communication skills includes seminars, facilitation, and training in listening effectiveness, organizational structure and change, and cultural diversity.

As a consultant and facilitator, she challenges and inspires substantive and engaging conversation by tapping into the knowledge, expertise, and experiences of participants and by raising their current perception of intra-personal communication to a new and even higher level. No one leaves a session without adding to his or her personal and professional toolbox.

BIBLIOGRAPHY

Borisoff, Deborah and Michael Purdy. *Listening in Everyday Life.* Maryland: University Press of America, 1997.

Burley-Allen, Madelyn. *Listening: The Forgotten Skill.* New York: Wiley, 1995.

Cormier, William and Sherry Cormier. *Interviewing Strategies for Helpers.* Monterey: Wadsworth, 1979.

DeVito, Joseph. *The Interpersonal Communications Book.* New York: Harper, 1992.

Eckman, Paul and Wallace Friesen. *Unmasking the Face.* New York: Prentice Hall, 1975.

Goss, Blaine and Dan O'Hair. *Communicating in Interpersonal Relationships.* New York: Macmillan, 1988.

Hahn, Martin and Scott Stoness. *Proceedings of the Twenty-First Annual Conference of the Cognitive Science Society.* London: Psychology Press, 1999.

Harris, Thomas and John Sherblom, John. *Small Group and Team Communication.* 4th ed. Pearson Education Inc, 2008.

Hirsch Jr, ed. *Cultural Literacy.* New York: Vintage, 1988.

Knapp, Mark. *Nonverbal Communication.* New York: Holt, Rinehart and Winston, 1978.

Medieval Life and Times. "Knights of the Round Table." *http://www.medieval-life-and-times.info/medieval-knights/knights-of-the-round-table.htm*

Krishnamurti, Jiddu. *First and Last Freedom.* New York: Harper and Row, 1975.

La Monica, Elaine. *La Monica Empathy Profile.* Tuxedo: Xicom, 1980.

Lakoff, George and Mark Johnson. *Metaphors We Live By.* Chicago: University of Chicago Press, 1980.

Maslow, Abraham. *Motivation and Personality.* New York: Harper and Row, 1954.

McKay, Matthew, Martha Davis, and Patrick Fanning. *Messages.* Oakland: New Harbinger, 1983.

Mehrabian, Albert. *Nonverbal Communication.* Chicago: Atherton Press, 1972.

Mehrabian, Albert. *Silent Message.* 2nd ed. Belmont: Wadsworth, 1981.

Nichols, Michael. *The Lost Art of Listening.* New York: Guilford Press, 1995,

Peck, M. Scott. *The Road Less Travelled.* New York: Simon and Schuster, 1978.

Sherman. "Listen with Your Heart." *Family Circle* Vol 111. February 17, 1998, 28.

Stohl, Cynthia. *Organizational Communication.* Thousand Oaks: Sage, 1995.

Thomlison, T. Dean. "Intercultural Listening." *Listening in Everyday Life.* Edited by Borisoff and M. Purdy. Maryland: University Press of America, 1997, 79–120.

Tubbs, Stewart and Sylvia Moss. *Human Communication.* Boston: McGraw Hill, 1994.

Wainwright, Gordan. *Body Language.* Boston: McGraw Hill, 1985.

Ward, John. *Now Hear This: Without Listening, There Is no Communication.* Communication World, v7, n7 (1990), 20–23.

Wells, Kenneth. *Guide to Good Leadership.* Chicago: Science Research Associates, 1956.

Wolvin, Andrew. *Listening and Human Communication in the 21st Century,* New York: Wiley, 2010.

Made in the USA
Columbia, SC
17 February 2020

87954666R00063